CAMPAIGNING
FOR CHANGE

*An Essential Guide
for Campaigning Around
the World*

Contents

Acknowledgements

I would like to thank all of the people who I have met across the world that I have campaigned with and trained, who have shown me that campaigning and a passionate desire to change the world is one element of our common humanity. You have all inspired me to do what I do and to write this book – thank you.

I will also always be grateful to Oxfam, the Empty Homes Agency, the Refugee Council and the British Red Cross for the amazing opportunities that they all offered to me to put my campaigning ideas into practice. And I will also always be grateful for the organisations across the world that have trusted me to train their people in campaigning – thank you.

In the writing of this book, I am grateful to Emma Taggart, Olivia Field, Brian Lamb and Ray Mitchell for their insightful comments on my draft text. In particular I am additionally grateful to Olivia Field for her detailed final edit on my draft text. And I am grateful to my brother, Graham, for showing me what is possible when you feel you have a book within you – thank you to you all.

Introduction

It is now a decade since I wrote my first book on campaigning, *Campaigning for success: how to cope if you achieve your campaign goal.* I was interested to note how driven I have become to write a second book. But this time, I wanted to reflect on how I have sought to enthuse people to campaign around the world, and to share some basic approaches, which seem to have resonated on my travels.

I wanted to go back to some of the campaigning tools, which I wrote about back in 2007. With the benefit of more campaigning experience and of endeavouring to inspire people around the globe to campaign, I have now developed 12 key questions that I feel you need to be able to answer before you can launch your campaign: your essential guide to campaigning.

These questions are meant to be a simple checklist, not too onerous at all, but a framework to help you to prepare your campaign. And these are the questions that I have used in my campaigning at a very practical level. Above all else, I would like to see these 12 simple questions de-mystify campaigning and show anyone who has that burning desire for change that campaigning is within their reach.

This simple checklist contains the key questions that you should be able to answer before you plunge into your campaign. I am interested that these questions have helped people in democratic contexts as well as in places where there is less freedom. I'd like to suggest that these 12 simple steps should be helpful no matter where you are in the world.

However you use this short book, whether you read all of it or just dip into it, I hope it helps you. Some things you will already know and some things I am sure you will dismiss – but if there is only one small nugget that helps you and spurs on your campaigning, then writing this book will be more than worthwhile.

I love to read or hear something that energizes me, makes me think, challenges me and makes me up my game – I hope there is something in this book that has that effect on you.

If you want to stay in touch with my latest thinking, do please visit my website: jonathanelliscampaigns.com. You may also be interested to know that I have designed on-line courses to complement this book on the Udemy training platform: https://www.udemy.com/user/jonathan-ellis-6/

Thanks for looking at my book and do let me know what you think.

Jonathan Ellis
Gladstone's Library, Hawarden
January 2017

1. What is campaigning and why is it important to you?

What is it that you actually do? This is the question that I have battled to answer over the past two decades since I got my first campaigning job with Oxfam. For me it was simple. I was a campaigner, I had always been a campaigner, and I just wanted to campaign against things that were not right, that were not just and not fair.

But I soon found that the word 'campaign' was a very loaded word in the English language. For some they will think only of party political campaigns, for others maybe an advertising or fundraising campaign. This is not what I meant by 'campaign'.

Some NGOs use advocacy as a better word to help people understand what they are trying to do – in my training I have taken an old definition of 'advocacy' from the Oxford English Dictionary: "*to recommend or support by argument a policy, cause . . .*"

Yet even this word doesn't always work. At the Red Cross we used the word 'advocacy' but this makes many people immediately think of lawyers or indeed, individual advocates for people such as in the Health Service. Again, not what we meant at all.

Over the years, maybe influenced by some of the approaches from across the Atlantic, I began to use the phrase 'advocacy campaign'.

I was mindful that you can have an 'election campaign', a 'fundraising campaign' or an 'advertising campaign' but neither the words 'campaign' nor 'advocacy' work alone.

I liked this term 'advocacy campaign'. My first manager when I took on a national role for Oxfam, Ian Chandler, has described advocacy campaigns as "a planned process to achieve change in institutional practice or public behaviour that will directly benefit affected communities (or causes)."

But in so many ways it does not matter at all what you call it but how you define it. For me advocacy campaigning is quite simple and can be broken down to this simple definition:

- Having a burning desire to see policy or practice change
- Identifying a clear problem and solution
- Knowing who has the power to make this change, what influences them and then seeking to influence them.

If you take nothing more from this book than these three bullet points, then I can rest easy. Having clarity on these three things will drive your campaign forward. And a lack of such clarity will hamper any effective campaigning.

Stripped to its basics, the rest of this book seeks to help you deliver on these three key points. It sounds so simple, but I have come across many a campaign that lacks clarity on these three simple points.

All of this takes me to my favourite stories that help people better understand campaigning:

The cookie story

The best definition of campaigning I have ever heard was given by a guy called Mark Latimer at a conference I attended many years ago. As I remember, after being asked how he would define campaigning, he invited the audience to picture the scene of a small girl at home in her kitchen with her mother.

The little girl had a problem: she was hungry. But she knew the solution to her problem: she wanted a cookie from her mother's cookie jar on the top shelf. She also knew that her mother had the power to give her one.

At first she tried the direct approach and said, "Mum, Mum, can I have a cookie?" Her mother said, "No".

She then said, "You gave me a cookie yesterday", so she was using historic precedent - she was a clever girl. Her mother still said, "No".

She then said, "You gave my little brother a cookie." Her mother again repeated, "The answer is no."

She then thought for a while and ran next door to the lounge where her father was watching television, and said, "Dad, Dad - Mum won't give me a cookie."

And that story is the most basic yet effective definition of campaigning I have ever heard. The little girl was:

- clear on the **problem**,
- she was very clear on the **solution** to that problem,

- she was also very clear who had the **power** to make the change she wanted to see
- and she then sought to **influence** that person.

Critical to this story is her focus and persistence - she didn't give up despite her initial failure.

When I ran a campaign training workshop in Tanzania a few years ago, their challenge at the end of the workshop was finding what their cookie was! To run an effective campaign you must know what your cookie is – or the change you really want to see happen.

The story over dinner

My other favourite campaigning story concerns a dinner I attended many years ago full of charity chief executives. I was sitting next to a charity chief executive, and when she found out what I did, she said to me very proudly that she wanted her charity to be a campaigning charity. I replied that that was great news, and asked her what her burning issue was.

She looked at me curiously, and said that she didn't have a burning issue, and that she just wanted to campaign. I replied that without a burning issue she wouldn't achieve success. She then didn't speak to me for the rest of the dinner.

I do think that campaigning is about having a burning desire to see change. And it is this desire that should compel us to campaign, not just a perception that we should be doing it!

Problem/solution/target/influence

When I think about campaigning, I try to keep it simple. It comes down to being clear on:

- the problem,
- the solution to that problem,
- who your target should be who has the power to make the change you want to see, and,
- how to influence that person.

I think campaigning is very much an art and not a science, and it is all about trying things, reflecting on your activity, and then trying something else all based on the best of your available evidence, intelligence and experience of the outside world, but not losing sight of these four key elements.

Real impact

So advocacy campaigns are about influencing people in positions of power to push for policy or practice change that will improve the lives of significant numbers of people.

And that last point is important. I remember years ago campaigning to end the scandal of England's empty homes. We had managed to secure a new power on empty property in the Housing Act 2004, and had begun to attend a series of meetings in Whitehall about the implementation of this new Act. I remember one of my colleagues at the time turning to me and challenging me saying, "you're enjoying all of this aren't you, but how many homeless families has this change in the law housed?"

And of course he was spot on. While the Act was on the Statute Book, not a single person had been able to move into a new home. On one level we had succeeded, but advocacy campaigns are meaningless unless you get a direct, tangible benefit for the very people you set out to help in the first place. And we should never lose sight of this truth. While we can seduce ourselves with the importance of commitments and new laws, unless things change on the ground none of this is important or, indeed relevant.

When I was at the Red Cross, I used to occasionally refer to my advocacy team as being a "walking opportunity cost", by which I meant that we could easily all be dismissed and the money used for frontline services. We needed to show that we were having an impact for our service users that our services alone could not achieve. To do this we needed more than just political commitments but real change on the ground. Now, this can take time, but the job is not done until this actually happens.

Services or campaigns?

Linked to this point is the age-old question often faced by campaigners in the voluntary sector: should we campaign or deliver direct services? I well remember this question being posed to me when I was at the Refugee Council.

Of course, the answer is both. In reality, services and campaigning should be mutually supportive. By delivering services you are acquiring real experience of the problem that your campaign should be seeking to address. You are responding directly to that need, but if your services alone are not enough to tackle the issue, then you do need to campaign to ensure that change comes about to address this problem.

This does not mean that campaigning groups have to deliver services; there are benefits and drawbacks to both services and campaigns being in the same organisation. The benefits are that you have the potential to gather operational evidence for your campaign. The drawbacks can be in a largely service-orientated organisation that campaigning may be a lower priority, and you may struggle to get your perspective understood and supported.

Yet if you are a campaigning organisation without direct services, then you will be well advised to have allies or connections with service providers to give you that direct operational experience to fuel your campaign.

Routes for advocacy campaigns

Another key question for any organisation is how you want your advocacy campaigns to be seen. This is sometimes crudely differentiated as the 'insider' or 'outsider' route.

Quite simply the 'insider' route seeks to use behind the scenes and non-public facing actions; while the 'outsider' route favours a public approach through, for example, demonstrations or the media.

How your organisation deals with this question is determined by:

- the organisation's desired positioning
- your understanding of the external context
- your understanding of the potential to influence your target

I remember years ago going to a Sheila McKechnie Foundation conference and hearing Kumi Naidoo give an inspiring talk on campaigning. He was asked which approach he favoured:

'insider' or 'outsider'? His response was classic – he favoured both approaches. But the critical thing was, in his opinion, that you should always keep your target guessing as to which approach you are going to use. No organisation should allow themselves to be pigeonholed into just one category of campaigning.

At the Red Cross, as an auxiliary to Government through the Geneva Convention, our default style was the insider route. But, we always reserved the right to go public when we felt we needed to exert extra pressure. And we did go public in my time on both the issues of First Aid being taught in schools and on refugee family reunion. In both cases, we felt there was a benefit in demonstrating public support on these issues.

TEA test

When it comes to seeking to influence your target, the person who you think has got the power to make the change you want to see, it is useful to think about whether you are passing the TEA test.

I developed this approach years ago when I went out to Senegal with Oxfam to help run a regional campaigns training workshop. Oxfam had just announced that it wanted to become a global campaigning force. We encountered a fair degree of resistance from colleagues in the region, who were somewhat wary of the word, 'campaigning.' It was then that I developed the idea of the TEA test to help my colleagues see that campaigning could also be relevant to them.

The TEA test stands for:

- **Touch** - you need to be able to touch and stir the soul of your target. But you need to do more than just touch you need to:
- **Enthuse** – show your target that change is possible and that there is a solution to your problem. Having touched *and* enthused your target, you then want to get that person to:
- **Act** – give them something to do to support your campaign.

I think the TEA test gives you a great framework when thinking about influencing someone. You are looking to **touch** them, to then move them on by **enthusing** them, all with a focus on getting them to **act**. Touch, enthuse and act – the TEA test.

I remember my former Oxfam colleagues in West Africa responding really well to the TEA test. While they may have had difficulties with the word 'campaigning', they proudly told me that they needed to pass the TEA test every day of their working lives. They were forever needing to touch, enthuse and get people to act – they had in fact been campaigning already.

It is a great idea to look at campaigns already out there and see whether they pass the TEA test for you. I am always interested when I come across a campaign that touches me, that enthuses me and then gets me to act.

What makes for a good advocacy campaign?

Over the years I have suggested that the following elements can make for a good advocacy campaign:

- **a clear and focussed message** - I like to talk about an absence of ambiguity with an effective campaign message.

- **a simple problem and solution** - I do love a good whinge, but I have also learnt that identifying a tangible solution is just so important.
- **clear outrage/ injustice** - this element is sometimes contested on my training courses, with some people uncomfortable with the notion of injustice. For me a campaign needs a real sense of something being wrong, unfair or outrageous to drive it forward. I don't think that being mildly irritated is the best catalyst for a campaign.
- **use of the media** - but only when the campaign needs it. I meet some campaigners who feel their campaign must always have media coverage. I think it is always good to question the need for media and not just to see it as a default position.
- **political support** - clearly this is important but there is a real danger of your issue being owned by one political party. You need to show that your issue is bigger than one party and is rooted in the evidence of the problem that you are facing.
- **alliances** - no matter how big you are - Oxfam or Red Cross for example - you can rarely push for change just by yourselves. I am always keen to promote thinking about possible 'surprising allies' and not just to focus on the usual suspects.
- **action** - an advocacy campaign needs action. People often think any campaigning action has to be a high-profile stunt; this is not the case. Sometimes the desired action might be something really small, like convincing the media or an MP to quote your campaign message. So long as an action builds momentum for your issue, size of the action doesn't matter.

- **people with real experience of your issue** - this is the holy grail for advocacy campaigning. The most effective lobbying I have ever witnessed was done by a young woman from the Democratic Republic of the Congo who tackled the then immigration minister on her lived experience of being an asylum seeker. To get to that point she had been supported by the Refugee Council, was supported during the encounter and again, afterwards.
- **momentum** - it is not enough to do just one thing, or have sporadic activity - you need to build sustained momentum and interest in your issue for change to happen.

What are the key mechanisms for advocacy campaigns?

When I am planning an advocacy campaign, I like to think about the following mechanisms and reflect on how I might use each of them as I develop my campaign:

- **research and analysis** - what evidence do you need to understand your issue and then fuel your campaign?
- **lobbying** - who do you need to get to directly to seek to influence?
- **media** - how can you use both traditional media and social media?
- **allies** - who can join you to add strength to your campaign? And it is always helpful to think about who might be a 'surprising ally' and not just the usual suspects.
- **public campaigning** - is it helpful to mobilise your supporters or the wider public for your campaign?

How policy change happens?

I was very taken several years ago when a former colleague from Oxfam, Chris Stalker, passed on to me the report, *Pathways for Change: 6 theories about how policy change happens,* by Organizational Research Services from the US.

While they have subsequently revised this report and included more theories, I much prefer their original version with the six theories of change. I just loved how they set out the full range of possible campaigning opportunities and conditions for each of the six approaches.

For me the key lesson is that change can happen in a number of different ways, and an effective campaigner needs to be open to all of the pathways no matter what may have worked for them in the past:

- **'Large Leap'** – where large-scale policy change is the goal. I think of the release of Nelson Mandela here, which then led to the first multi-racial elections in South Africa.
- **'Coalition theory'** – co-ordinated activity among a range of individuals with the same core belief. My most successful campaigning on refugee issues, as you'll see later, only occurred when we built a wide coalition of not just the usual suspects.
- **'Policy windows'** – advocates using a window of opportunity to push a policy solution. This makes me think of how campaigners in the UK used the opportunity of the Government ending the immigration detention of children to push for an end to adult immigration detention.

- **'Messaging and frameworks'** – the key issue for influence is how issues are framed and presented. With the campaign to end smoking in public places, a key turning point was the decision to frame the message as a health and safety at work issue for restaurant staff.
- **'Power Politics'** – where policy change is achieved by working directly with those with power. When I was campaigning on empty homes, we went straight to the Housing Minister, and in passing the TEA test with him, we began to get his support for action on empty homes.
- **'Community organising theory'** – where policy change happens through the collective action of the members of a community who work on changing problems affecting their own lives. I just love what living wage campaigners have achieved in the UK by tackling company by company to address poverty pay.

What qualities do you need to be an effective campaigner?

Having tested this list around the world, I do think the following qualities are helpful:

- **passion** - showing that you really care about your issue,
- **persistence** - not giving up, just like the little girl after a cookie,
- **vision of what you are going to achieve** - what does the world look like when you have achieved your campaign goal?
- **flexibility** - it may not be in your plan but having the ability to respond to opportunities to strengthen your campaign whilst retaining your focus,

- **creative use of campaigning tools** - how you are using research, lobbying, media, allies and public campaigning in ways that help your campaign,
- **curiosity about power and influence** - really wanting to know who has the power to make things happen and how they can be influenced,
- and above all

  a burning desire for change

  and **a sense of enjoyment!**

2. What is your problem? But why is it a problem?

Campaign Focus

Over the last decade I have been fortunate enough to travel around the world supporting the development of advocacy campaigns. One of my consistent themes is the need for focus. I remember running a workshop in Warsaw where the NGO representatives proudly listed their 27 campaign priorities. I challenged them, saying 27 issues were just too many – I can barely remember 27 different things! They needed much greater focus.

As a student in the UK in the 1980s, I remember listening to Neil Kinnock asking questions of Margaret Thatcher when she was Prime Minister. On one occasion that still haunts me, he asked her a shopping list length of questions in just one slot. Of course she could then decide which, if any, of them, she would choose to answer. For me focus in advocacy campaigns is an absolute priority.

A politician would just love you to come to her or him with 27 things. Instead, focus and persistence are key factors for effective advocacy campaigns.

Selecting your priority

But how do you decide your priority issue? I recall my colleagues in Warsaw asking me that question. I think that a critical issue here is having the courage to pick an issue to start you off; once you develop some momentum and success, you can then turn to other issues, but until then have the courage to pick your initial focus.

As I have delivered my training courses, and this issue of focus has come up, I would routinely say that I have no interest in what issue they were to select, but I would have a paramount interest in how they reached their decision. The selection criteria for advocacy campaigns are critical.

In my training I have suggested a number of possible selection criteria to help people decide their priority focus for an advocacy campaign. These include:

- experience and evidence
- clear solution
- 'winnability' - is the solution actually achievable?
- views of people with real experience of your issue
- interest from your target.

During my time at the Refugee Council in the UK, I was asked to lead the process to decide our priority campaign issues. In so doing, I suggested that the key selection criterion should be injustice. Having clear selection criteria was absolutely vital when I was later challenged on the final priorities of destitution, detention and legal support. People may not have agreed with the final choice, but with transparent criteria they could see how the choice had been made. I do think that transparent selection criteria for your advocacy campaign are so important.

But why?

I have also come to see how important it is to really understand the problem that your advocacy campaign is seeking to address. Are you really going to tackle the problem or just its superficial appearance?

From my time running advocacy training courses for INTRAC (the International Training and Research Centre), I became very well acquainted with one of their key tools – the 'but why?' technique.

In addition to the cookie story, the 'but why?' technique shows why very often it is children who are really the best campaigners. I remember as a young boy being told by my mother to stop asking "why?" the whole time. As campaigners we should forever be asking why – we should carry an instinctive curiosity with us.

With this tool, you take your problem and someone, ideally with no knowledge of your issue, asks you, "but why?" You then answer that question. You are then asked, "but why?" And you try to answer again, and so it continues.

At INTRAC a number of us trainers used this hypothetical example. It is a bit simplistic, but it does make the point soundly about the need to ask, "but why?"

'But why?' in action

The immediate problem

The children are not going to school
  • **But why?**

- They keep falling ill
    Possible response: provide medicines

- **But why?**
- They drink bad water
    Possible response: dig a well

- **But why?**
- The well is too far from the school
    Possible response: put in a pipe

- **But why?**
- The local government said it would dig a new well last year but it hasn't
    Possible response: dig a well or lobby local government

- **But why?**
- The government has not released the funds that are supposed to have been set aside
    Possible response: dig a well/put in a pipe or lobby central government

- **But why?**
- The bilateral donors haven't released the pledged aid funds
    Possible response: dig a well/put in a pipe or lobby bilateral donors

This simple example shows that there may be responses to this problem at a number of different levels from providing humanitarian support by supplying medicines to lobbying the bilateral donors.

In my time at the Red Cross we were keen to turn attention to the problem of destitute people, who had been refused refugee status but were unable to be returned home. We used the "but why?" technique to help us focus down on the real problem that we needed to address as opposed to just talking about destitution in general.

- Asylum seekers are destitute – but why?
- They have been refused refugee status but cannot return home – but why?
- There are some countries that people cannot be returned to – but why?
- These countries are too dangerous to fly into or do not accept people back who have fled – but why?
- The government refuses to accept this is the case for a limited number of countries – but why?
- The government has not been forced to focus on these countries and produce a policy response – but why?
- There has been no focused pressure on this point

We therefore commissioned research on this niche issue so that we could exert focused pressure to push for policy change.

I also did this exercise in South Africa, and one of the participants asked me what he should do when he found that one of his answers was "maybe this and maybe that"? I replied that his uncertainty showed he was not yet ready to launch a campaign. He needed more evidence to develop his understanding of the problem.

Of course there is always a danger that this exercise never stops and one keeps on being asked: "but why?" But it is a great way to test your understanding of the problem your campaign is seeking to address. You may well come out with answers at different levels.

I have seen this tool be highly effective for campaigning alliances, where different alliance members have taken on responsibility for different answers to the 'but why?' exercise.

This campaign tool should come with a major health warning: it can be profoundly irritating to be asked "but why?" repeatedly on an issue about which you are passionate. Yet it can be hugely helpful to you to ensure that you really get to the root cause of the problem, and ensure that your solution will really address the problem.

I have also found that politicians and journalists are very adept at asking "but why?" This technique also helps you prepare and work through your answers.

3. Is there a common understanding of your external environment?

Having a common understanding of your external environment is just so important in ensuring you have a robust foundation for your advocacy campaign.

As I have run training workshops around the world, I have tried to give ever more time for this exercise at the start of each workshop. I recall once being in Dhaka running a South East Asia regional workshop for a Swiss NGO. I broke the workshop into their country groupings to discuss their external environment and to produce a poster to describe what it's like to the other groups.

All of the Asian countries went off and began their discussions, but the colleagues from Switzerland kicked back, and said that there was little point them doing this exercise as they all had the same opinion already. I asked them to indulge me and try the exercise. I went back to them half an hour later to find them having a robust exchange. They did not have the same opinion after all. There is such a danger in assuming that everyone on the team shares the same understanding of the external world.

It is good to test that assumption and write down your shared understanding; then as your campaign develops and your intelligence grows deeper, you should review and update your assessment of the external environment.

Again, I did this exercise with colleagues from Ethiopia; there was a heated discussion and I think in the end an agreement to disagree. Yet all of those involved in the discussion commented that it had been helpful to air their differences, and not just blindly build a strategy assuming a common understanding.

Another example I won't forget is running a workshop for some senior and experienced legal people in the UK. We were discussing an issue and I asked them who they thought had the power to make the change they wanted to see. They skirted around the issue but it soon became very clear that they just did not know who had the power. We resolved to undertake some political intelligence work to develop their understanding. Yet if this question had not been posed, we may have launched a campaign without actually knowing who the real target for the campaign was!

I think that there are just a few simple questions that can help you make your assessment of the external environment:

- how does change happen in your society?
- where does power lie in your society? And more specifically who has the power on your issue?
- where does influence lie in your society? And more specifically, who has influence over those with power on your issue?
- what influencing approaches have worked in this environment on those in power?
- How are you answering your curiosity about power and influence?

I used to, on occasion, use a framework developed by the World Bank for helping people to develop their assessment of space for civil society (*The World Bank ARVIN Framework: A Way to Assess the*

Enabling Environment for Civic Engagement); while some people found this approach helpful, I began to think it was offering too rigid a structure. I wanted people to have more freedom to think about, discuss and describe how change happens and where power lies.

If we don't have a robust understanding of our external world, we do run the risk of running fantasy advocacy campaigns. While they may be beautifully crafted, using all the techniques listed in the pages to follow, if they have no basis or grounding in the political reality, they are no better than just fantasy. With limited time and resources, there is no room for fantasy; our plans must be rooted in reality of our world.

4. What evidence have you got or do you need?

The fuel for effective advocacy campaigns is undoubtedly evidence. You really need to be able to show the evidence of the problem that your campaign is seeking to address.

I should just add a few words of warning. The need for comprehensive research can be one of the most effective delaying tactics for campaigning. You may have identified a real problem and then commission a two-year research project, by which time the issue will have surely moved on.

Indeed at Oxfam when we were campaigning against the unjust asylum voucher scheme (which denied asylum seekers cash support giving them vouchers which could only be used at a limited number of stores and no change was given), we launched our campaign with practically no evidence base at all but just a sense of wanting to speak out against this injustice impacting on vulnerable people. And I am pleased that we did not wait, as the issue needed an immediate response. (We would then, several months later, work on our evidence base that then served to energise the momentum we had already built up).

At the Red Cross I came into post extolling the virtues of 'quick and dirty' research to fuel our advocacy work. I soon realised that my research colleagues found this term quite insulting to their professional status! We compromised on the phrase, 'rapid and revealing' which, in addition to great alliteration, also captured my intent for the research perfectly. We wanted our evidence to be rapid as there was a need for speed but also revealing to show the need for our solutions.

For me there are several key points that one needs to address when thinking about evidence for your advocacy campaign:

- what evidence of your problem do you have?
- what does the 'but why?' technique tell you that you need by way of evidence?
- does the evidence already exist?
- be wary – research can be the greatest excuse for not campaigning!
- rapid and revealing – ideally macro and micro – numbers and human stories
- who is going to do it – you, an ally, or an independent researcher?

5. Do you pass the TEA test with your solution?

I think the TEA test, as outlined in section 1 above, is a great way of assessing an advocacy campaign. When campaigns communicate with me via post or email, I am always interested to see if they pass the TEA test with me – touching me, enthusing me and then getting me to take an action.

Years ago Action Aid UK wrote to me about the state of farmers in South Africa working to supply a UK chain of supermarkets. Their message was that these farmers were being forced to live in poverty, but for an increase of only 5p an hour, their lives could be transformed. Action Aid then asked their supporters to find a 5p piece, stick it to their postcard and send it on to the supermarket's chief executive.

I was interested to find myself doing just that – their pitch resonated with me and they certainly passed the TEA test – they had touched me, enthused me and then got me to act. A month or so later, Action Aid wrote back to me saying that the supermarket had agreed to increase the hourly rate of these farmers. What a great result – passing the TEA test with their supporters and making a difference on the ground.

The TEA test in action

I remember years ago having the opportunity to meet the Minister of State for Justice to discuss Red Cross concerns about the withdrawal of publicly funded legal support for refugee family reunion. He was very clear at the start of the meeting that the Government did not agree with our concerns, but he gave me the space to make my case.

I endeavoured to convey the argument that refugee family reunion is not an issue of immigration but one of international protection for refugees. I sought to explain that very often, it would be one member of the family, most often the male, who is able to reach a safe country, and then he or she will seek to use refugee family reunion procedures to bring the rest of the family to safety. The importance of this re-unification is to ensure the on-going protection of all the family members.

It was only when I started telling the minister about a story that I had heard about a brother and sister being physically separated in a refugee camp that I felt I was beginning to touch him. It was a harrowing tale of their hands slipping out of each other's grasp, and the brother then losing sight of the sister. It was at this point that the minister's interest grew. He then promised me a subsequent meeting with his officials to discuss what might be possible.

I felt that I had touched him with my story, enthused him that change was possible, and then before I left the meeting got him to commit to act. In this instance I felt I passed the TEA test. Admittedly this was just the start - but this meeting had got us up and running.

Does your campaign pass the TEA test? Are you touching, enthusing and then getting your target to act?

6.   Can you do the elevator pitch?

The elevator pitch is a bit of fun, but if you get it right, it will form an effective foundation for your advocacy campaign.

Imagine, if you will, that you enter an elevator (or lift)...

The one politician you have been waiting months to speak to steps into the elevator with you.

How do you use the next 15-30 seconds?

I suggest that you would need clarity on your elevator pitch for those precious few seconds. In addition to introducing yourself, you need to cover:

- your problem
- your solution
- your ask

In talking about your problem you might cover:

- what problem is your campaign focussed on?
- where is your evidence?
- can you distil your problem into a few words?

And for your solution:

- what needs to happen for this problem to be tackled?

- how do you know?
- can you distil your solution into a few words?

Having covered your problem and your solution, and if your target is still with you, you then need to be clear: what is your ask? And your ask might be as simple as could we arrange to meet? Or would you read our research report on the issue?

Remember to bear in mind the importance of …

- Practice
- Practice
- Practice

So that you never knowingly lose a chance to make your pitch and you are always ready. When I have been running a campaign for a while, my elevator pitch gets smoother and quicker. It may sound easy but it is not easy to do well. You really do need to practice your pitch so that it becomes effortless.

It is superb to have your pitch ready for when you meet a politician, an ally or do a media interview. It means you are quickly out of the blocks and do not have to spend time thinking about how to start. The elevator pitch is a great foundation stone for an effective campaign.

Elevator pitch examples from my time at the Red Cross

Hi! I'm Jonathan from the Red Cross. We are concerned that at best only one in five schools teach their children basic first aid techniques. We don't think that's enough. We'd like to see every child given the chance to learn first aid so that we see a generation of lifesavers. We think we could do more. Would you meet with me to discuss how we might make this happen?

Hi! I'm Jonathan from the Red Cross. We are concerned that you can't get a short-term wheelchair loan on the NHS. If you break your leg, your ability to get a wheelchair loan should not depend upon whether the Red Cross runs a voluntary service locally. We think everyone should have the right to a short-term loan. Would you meet with me to discuss how we might work together to identify the unmet need across the country?

Hi! I'm Jonathan from the Red Cross. We have become increasingly worried about the impact of the withdrawal of publicly funded legal support for refugee family reunion - families ripped apart by conflict. We know how complex this process can be and how vital legal support is for these families. We think that there should be publicly funded legal support for refugees with permission to stay in the UK to be re-united with their immediate pre-flight family. Would you meet with me to discuss how we might work together to help these families?

7. How credible are you and what are the risks?

Credibility

When your campaign starts rolling, and you begin to build momentum and interest, you will inevitably at some stage find yourself under attack. One key angle of attack against any campaigner is on their credibility. As you develop your campaign, it is really important that you consider your answers to these two questions:

- what makes you credible to speak out on your issue?
- where do you get your mandate?

At the Red Cross we were always clear that our credibility to speak out on refugee issues came from our operational experience on the ground supporting refugees in 60 locations across the UK; we maintained that this operational footprint and our conversations with our service users all gave us a mandate to speak out.

Risks

Campaigners should also be ready to face any risks arising from their campaign. I've found the following points helpful in managing risks on my campaigns:

- listing and understanding the risks of your campaigning
- you must then take ownership of your risks and not let others do so for you

- use a risk register to identify the risks, their likelihood and likely impact and the actions you will take to reduce these risks
- review this register as part of your campaign planning

The more I campaign, the more I think that the people running the campaign should take ownership of all the potential risks. They should list them, confront them and show how they are going to reduce any likely impact. I think that campaigners should own these risks and not allow other people to own them. If other people own them, they are better able to stall or even block the campaign.

Any good advocacy campaign strategy should have a risk assessment as an embedded element. Such a risk assessment should list all of the potential risks from the campaign, and then assess with a score the potential impact of this risk and its chance of actually happening. Then the associated action to reduce the likelihood of this risk should be included.

Here's an example of an advocacy campaign risk assessment:

Risk	Likelihood (1 low–4 high)	Impact (1 low–4 high)	Action to reduce the risk
Campaign is embraced by just one political party	2	4	Ensure there is engagement with all of the political parties

Lack of support from own supporters for campaign	1	3	Ensure regular communication with supporters in run-up to launch and then on-going responses to any concerns
Attack in the media about campaign	2	4	Develop good network of allies who will be ready to speak out publicly in defence of the campaign

Too often I have seen campaigners put all of their energy into developing a campaign plan and submit for approval to the senior management team or trustees. And the ensuing feedback asks about risks. Here, risks are seen as being owned by senior management or trustees. Instead, the campaigners should be taking ownership of the risks right from the outset, not shying away from them, and being explicit about how they are going to reduce them.

We should be clear that any activity of daily human life has risks; advocacy campaigning is no different. So therefore we should take ownership of these risks, not defer to others and keep the risk assessment under regular review.

8. Do you know who your target is and how to reach them?

The Influence tree

One of the earliest campaign tools that I learnt was the influence tree. In undertaking this exercise, you need to be able to respond to the following points:

- who has the power to make the change you want to see?
- who influences that person?
- how can you seek to influence those people to influence your target?
- and never forget the direct route! Going back to the cookie story, you should always try to go directly to the person who has the power to make the change you want to see.

In the diagram, your target is placed at the top of the tree. Your influence tree shows the different routes to influence your target, and one route will be the direct route. You need to ponder: what are the other routes you could go down? This is one time that you need to apply your creative thinking to your campaign. And remember that an influence tree is the road map for your campaign.

To create an influence tree, at the top of a piece of paper in a box you list the target that you are seeking to influence. (See the influence tree in theory below)

Underneath this box you then create a number of boxes into which you write the names of people or organisations that you know have influence over the target. One of the boxes should be yourself because the direct approach to achieving change is always important: at the very least to try to go directly to your target.

But the critical thing about the influence tree is thinking about the number of different roads you could go down to influence your target. A critical part of this technique is having intelligence as to what influences your target.

What do you know of the person you are seeking to influence? What organisations or people are they influenced by or which media do they look at? A critical part of successful campaigning is having an instinctive curiosity about the person you are trying to influence.

Sometimes you will initially realise that you don't know enough, and that you have got to go out and get some more intelligence from other people. The critical thing is thinking about the different roads go down to seek influence, if the direct approach does not work.

An important lesson I have learnt about effective influencing very much comes down to knowledge and access. Sometimes one might have the knowledge but not the access, and sometimes you have the access but not the knowledge. With campaigning if you have the knowledge but not the access, you need to find a sympathetic person or organisation to help you get the access to make sure your knowledge is heard as you seek to influence.

Influence Tree in theory

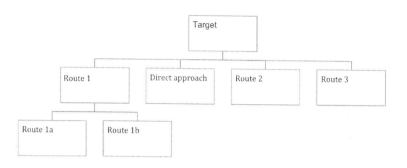

Influence Tree in practice

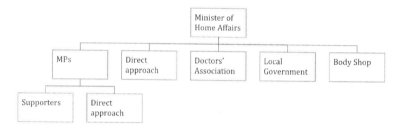

In this practical example, we were trying to influence the Minister of State at the Home Office to abolish the supermarket voucher scheme for asylum seekers and replace them with cash support. We initially wrote to the Minister who refused to meet us. We then sought other routes to influence him. Our varied routes to our target began to show, over time, that there was growing support from diverse parts of society for change on this issue.

It was helpful to have the voices heard from cross-party Members of Parliament on this issue. We also gained support from the Doctor's Association expressing their concern about the health implications of this policy and the Local Government Association expressing their concerns about the implications for local councils. The Body Shop was our 'surprising ally' who expressed their support for our campaign and then ran their own campaign on this issue in some of their shops. Over time we began to show the growing support for change on this issue.

9. How are you using opposition to help you?

One important element of campaigning, that I didn't give much attention to until relatively recently, is the central importance of opposition. When I was younger I was very uninterested in opposition to my campaigns. Put simply I was right and they were wrong. But as I got older and began to gain more experience, I began to realise that the opposition to my campaign was like gold dust. It should be cherished, and studied closely. If I feel strongly about something, then I should be instinctively interested in the opposition and in what was blocking that change from happening.

Another useful campaigning tool is the opposition matrix. Again this is a very simple tool - take a blank sheet of paper and draw a line down the middle. On the left-hand side list all of the arguments against your campaign. This can be quite a sobering exercise, and is best done in a group. On the other side of the page, list all of the arguments in favour of your campaign. See the opposition matrix in theory below.

Then reflecting and looking at the arguments against your campaign, really begin to think whether you are actually addressing your opponents' arguments in your campaign messages.

One thing I have seen very often, and this is certainly my own experience, is that as campaigners we very often choose the messages that motivate ourselves. Campaigning is not about motivating ourselves, as we should hopefully already be motivated. It is about choosing the most effective method and message to tackle the arguments of your opponents. The opposition matrix can be a really useful way to think about opposition, and then to reflect on the most powerful messages that you can choose to marshal in order to tackle this opposition.

A critical action here is anticipation of opposition on your issue. The opposition matrix can help you to anticipate and hence then to prepare for any opposition arguments. As a campaigner it is also vital that you try to see your issue from your target's perspective. Why are they opposed? And what might they need to hear or see to help them engage?

Opposition Matrix in theory

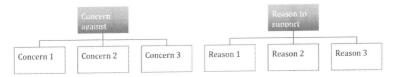

Opposition matrix in action

Empty Homes

When I was at the Empty Homes Agency, we ran a campaign to promote the need for new powers for local authorities to take on compulsory leases of long-term empty property, where there was no good reason for them being empty to help meet housing need. Our opposition matrix on that issue looked like this:

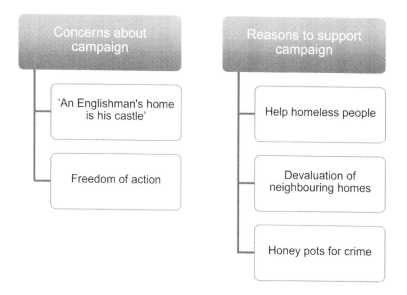

When I did this exercise for the first time, I realised that my key argument for the campaign, namely to help homeless people, just did not address the concerns about the campaign. Yet it was only when I started to use arguments of devaluation of neighbouring homes and of attracting crime to the area that I began gain new support. An English man's home may be his 'castle', but if his actions or inaction impact on another person's 'castle' by devaluing it or attracting crime to the area, then that is a problem.

It was sobering to realise that my chosen campaign message on homelessness was not nearly as effective in winning over sceptics as the other messages at my disposal. This experience showed me the importance of the opposition matrix and of thinking very hard about my chosen campaign message.

Right to work

When I was at the Refugee Council I was involved in running a campaign with the Trades Union Congress (TUC) calling for asylum seekers to be given the right to work. In 1986, the Government had given asylum seekers the right to work, but this right had been taken away in 2002. Asylum seekers were often criticised for taking state benefits, but many people did not realise that they did not have the right to work. We sought to change this state of affairs.

On this issue, our opposition matrix looked like this:

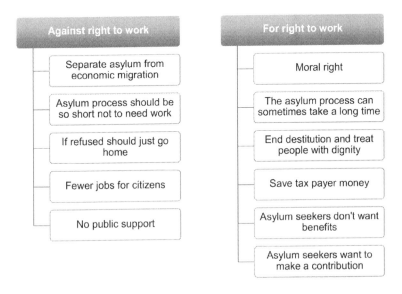

Once again undertaking this exercise was a sobering experience for me. We had been running with the key messages around the moral right and the need to end destitution and treat people with dignity, but we were not engaging with the politicians that we needed to in order to gain more support in Parliament on this issue. Yet when we moved onto other issues, such as saving taxpayers money, we began to build support.

A few years ago I ran a workshop where I was explaining the opposition matrix, and I remember being accused by a young woman of selling out on my principles by using this approach. I don't think so at all. I am not saying that you drop your key arguments. On empty homes I would always talk at some stage about homelessness and on the right to work about dignity, there would just be some occasions when I would choose not to lead on these messages.

What I want is for my message to be heard by my target, and that often means starting in a different place for them to begin to engage with me. Campaigning is about human relationships and finding the best way to engage with your target, and not just repeating the messages that motivate you as a campaigner. Campaigning is about getting real change – not just communicating about the need for change.

I have always said to my teams, when you are campaigning your messages must be consistent, and if every one of your engagements were to be played back to you, there has to be some consistency. What the opposition matrix does, however, is encourage you to reflect on which message might be the best one to lead with for maximum impact.

When I am campaigning, what is important to me is to build support and secure change on my issue. If that means leading on different messages to build that support, then I will happily do that. My messaging is not about appealing to my convictions, but about building support – that is why I think this tool is so useful.

At the Red Cross, we would use the opposition matrix before we had major meetings such as with Government ministers. When we did this preparation, I would go into these meetings with a great sense that I was ready and primed for anything – I do recommend using it to prepare for such meetings.

10. Have you got a theory of change?

Another critical part of effective campaigning is gaining momentum. I have been to so many campaign launches where an impressive report has been published, and great speeches made with maybe some subsequent media work, but then nothing happens as a result.

The critical element is momentum. There's a lot of talk in the campaigning world about theory of change. Sometimes this talk over complicates what should be a very simple process. When I think about a theory of change, I think about doing something **so that** something else happens **so that** something else happens **so that** something else happens and so on.

In short, you do something **so that** something else happens. No activity should exist by itself. Where you get real impact with campaigning one activity leads to another activity and the pressure for change builds. Those two little words – '**so**' and '**that**' – are so important to campaigners, and will help you to stay focused.

I sometimes call this approach a 'so that chain' – this is how I understand a theory of change. It is your theoretical approach to achieving change that you are going to put to the test, review, adapt, and keep pushing forward.

For example: I commissioned some research **so that** I have the evidence of the problem; **so that** I can brief politicians; **so that** they can raise the issue with government; **so that** I can hear where the government stands; **so that** I can modify my position; **so that** I can be more effective; **so that** I can push a policy change.

A critical element of campaigning is seeing where your activity goes, and will ultimately lead, and not just focusing on one activity in isolation. Yet it is also important to start from scratch – what is the very first action you need to take so that what happens?

But you should also never lose sight of the ultimate destination for your theory of change; you should never lose sight of what success should look and feel like, how you will tackle your problem, and how your actions will take you there.

Looking back over my campaigning, I have always had a theory of change in my head. But it is vital you write it down, share it with others, be open to challenge and see it as your guiding document.

It takes courage to write down your theory of change as none of us can see into the future. But you do so based on the best intelligence you have at the time and then being open to challenge and review.

A theory of change, together with a compelling message of problem and solution, can be invaluable in building support for your campaign. And it can be hugely helpful in attracting funding as you are showing how you think change is going to happen on your issue.

I also think it can be so powerful to share your general theory of change (or you might call it 'your direction of travel') with your supporters. I must confess that I tire of being sent the occasional email action or postcard action – "share your theory of change with me, show me where you think you are going", I say, so that I can understand where your campaign is going and where my action fits in!

I remember doing some campaign training in Nigeria many years ago and one of the people on the course said to me that he had learnt nothing new from my campaigning tools! But he did add that he had learnt the critical importance of seeing things strategically, seeing how activities joined up and not being content with doing something, stopping, and then picking up a bit later. For him his key learning was campaigning was all about **momentum**.

In terms of developing a theory of change, it may be helpful to think of....

- **big steps:** We are going to do some research; so that we can build allies; so that we all promote our issue to government; so that they respond; so that the policy is changed...
- **small steps:** we are going to develop a terms of reference; so that we can commission a researcher; so that we can plan a research plan; so that....

But remember . . .

"No battle plan ever survives the first contact with the enemy" (Helmut von Moltke)

Therefore you need to review your advocacy campaign regularly. One discipline that I endeavoured to introduce during my time at the Red Cross was the importance of the monthly review meeting for our three priority advocacy issues.

At these monthly review meetings, there should be just one agenda item: your theory of change. You should review the progress made on your 'so that' chain or theory of change. If you have got stuck, why have you got stuck? What have you learnt about getting stuck? And what changes are you going to make to your theory of change?

Over a twelve-month period, you should then have twelve different theories of change recorded, which will chart the thinking and progress of your campaign. This tool can be invaluable in monitoring your advocacy campaign.

Story telling

The more that I have campaigned, and developed theories of change for my issues; the more I have begun to see how important story telling is to a campaigner.

When I am promoting an advocacy campaign, I like to see it as a story:

- Where have we come from?
- Where are we now?
- Where are we going in the future?

I think that campaigners need to craft their own story using the past, present and future. And I do not mean being a passive storyteller. I mean being an active story maker – the essence of campaigning.

The effective campaigner with a strong campaign message needs to be an effective story teller to build support for their campaign – to tell their story of where they have come from, where they are now and how change is going to happen. Campaigners need to embrace the ancient art of story telling but seeing themselves as an active part of that story going forward.

For example towards the end of my time at the Red Cross, my campaign story was something like this ....

Where have we come from?

Over the past 3 years we have been advocating to end the scandal of asylum destitution in the UK. Firstly we started gathering evidence on the problem of refugees granted permission to stay in the country but then finding themselves destitute. Based on our evidence we convinced the government to make a number of policy and practice changes.

Where are we now?

We are now collecting evidence of the problem of people denied refugee status but who are unable to be returned home.

Where are we going in the future?

We will be using this evidence in the future to ensure that no-one is stuck in limbo unable to be returned home with neither the right to support or work leaving them open to abuse and exploitation.

Theory of change in action

Here are two theories of change that show how some of my early campaigns took off to build momentum leading to policy and practice change:

Campaign by Oxfam to abolish the use of supermarket vouchers to support asylum seekers and to re-introduce support in the form of cash (2000-1)

In 2000 the then Labour Government introduced a new system to provide support for asylum seekers waiting for a decision on their asylum application. From 1ˢᵗ April asylum seekers would no longer receive their support in the form of cash, but in vouchers redeemable at a restricted number of supermarkets, and when these vouchers were used, asylum seekers were not permitted to receive change. In addition there were growing fears that this voucher scheme was making it easier to identify asylum seekers and therefore encouraging discrimination.

Issue press statement in opposition to vouchers with our partners

So that

We establish our concern and intent

So that

We can launch a campaign action with the Refugee Council targeted at supermarkets to show customer opposition to this scheme

So that

We use this initiative to seek support of leading trade union leader Bill Morris of the TGWU (now UNITE) to use his quote on our postcard

So that

We can distribute cards across the country to get campaign going

So that

We then develop a dossier of disgrace to show the humanitarian impact of the voucher scheme across the country for the TGWU to use in their meetings with the Government

So that

We work with the TGWU on a fringe meeting at TUC conference and on a conference motion condemning the voucher scheme

So that

We build momentum at Labour conference for a motion against the voucher scheme

So that

The Government announces they will launch a review of the voucher scheme

So that

We utilise the success of getting a review of the voucher scheme to commission our own research into the impact of the voucher scheme

So that

We launch our report - *Token Gestures* in Parliament

So that

We launch our new campaign action based on our research findings targeting MPs

So that

We work with the British Medical Association on promoting the health impact of vouchers on asylum seekers

So that

We work with the Body Shop to develop a campaign in some of their shops (and in some Oxfam shops too)

So that

We work with Bill Morris to promote the need for change in the media

So that

We encourage support for a motion against vouchers at Labour conference

So that

The Home Secretary announces in Parliament that the voucher scheme will be scrapped and cash support re-introduced

So that

The voucher scheme is scrapped and cash re-introduced for all asylum seekers.

Campaign by Empty Homes Agency to promote the need for new powers for local authorities to tackle long-term empty property to help address housing need (2002-6)

Do reactive media work in response to stories on the housing crisis to promote need for action on private empty property

So that

At meeting with Housing Minister we promote the need for action on private empty property

So that

We pass the TEA test and get his agreement to launch a consultation on new powers

So that

We continue to promote the need for new powers at every opportunity in the media

So that

The Minister sets up a consultation on the issue

So that

We encourage positive responses to the government consultation

So that

We continue to make the case to government for action

So that

We meet with cross-party MPs to ensure the case for new powers is made from across the House

So that

We utilise opportunity of Housing Bill to ensure amendments raised from across the House

So that

We keep talking to officials so that they are briefed on possible policy options

So that

An amendment is successfully passed to Housing Bill

So that

We keep talking to officials on finer details

So that

We keep making the case for change in the media directly and with partners

So that

We join the Housing Act implementation group once the Bill gains Royal Assent

So that

We offer support to Local Authorities in using the new powers

So that

We celebrate the first local authority to use the new power to help address housing need.

11. Have you got a plan for success?

Coping with campaign success

I never cease to be amazed that, while campaigners will have their campaign plan, it very rarely includes what they will do in the event of their campaign succeeding.

Firstly, I think that it is important to give your target time and space to move – do not close off their channels as they seek to change position. You must think through: how is your target going to be able to change course, and what do you need to do to help that change to happen?

It is important to try to see your issue from your target's perspective. Sometimes it is hard to admit you have changed your mind, especially in public. You need to be thinking about how you can help ensure your target has room to move, and that there is a clear exit route, enabling your target to embrace the new policy or practice.

At your moment of breakthrough - when your target finally agrees with your pitch, you need to:

Have a plan for success. How will you now deal with your target? Will you walk away or will you work with them to shape the detail? How will you engage with your allies and the media at this moment? You may have gained a commitment but no real action. How do you turn that commitment into action on the ground?

And I firmly believe that the answer is that you never stop campaigning – at this point of success you are at your most vulnerable. Once your issue becomes the established policy, you may well find yourself being campaigned against. You need to continue to make the case for change at the moment of breakthrough.

I feel I have made some of my biggest mistakes as a campaigner when I have achieved that moment of breakthrough. Indeed back in 2007, I wrote a book on this very subject *Campaigning for Success - how to cope if you achieve your campaign goal* (NCVO).

Once your target begins to agree with your campaign message, you need to be clear about how you are going to:

- **conduct yourself with your target** – will you give full support, become a critical friend or push even harder?
- **deal with the media** – how will you present yourself once it seems you and your target are beginning to share the same view on an issue?
- **communicate with your allies** – they may assume it is all over for the campaign. How do you keep them involved and interested in case you need their support later?

Critically, you need to plan for success and you should never stop campaigning.

12. When are you next going to review progress?

And finally the best-made plan is worth nothing unless it is reviewed on a regular basis. As I've already mentioned when I was at the Red Cross, I tried with varying degrees of success to instigate a monthly review for each of our three advocacy priorities.

The idea for this review meeting was simply to review the theory of change. To recap: you look at what you have done - how many 'so thats' you have achieved. If you have got stuck, you explore why and what changes are now needed to be made to the theory of change? And where there have been external engagements over the period, think about what these have told you about any necessary changes to your theory of change?

So after each meeting, you should come out with a revised theory of change, which then becomes your action plan for the next period. And indeed if you meet monthly, you should keep a record of each monthly theory of change, as it should prove very helpful in monitoring the campaign.

And there will be some periods where your campaign will move so fast that you will need to review progress much more often. And I always find when you meet with a key decision maker that there are always implications for your theory of change, and you should have a review meeting after each such engagement.

But the essence is to develop your plan, engage with the outside world, review your plan and keep going building momentum as you push for your desired policy or practice change. It sounds so easy but is hard to do on a sustained basis – so keep the focus, avoid too many internal distractions, and keep pushing for that end goal!

In conclusion

So that's it - it does sound so simple doesn't it? It may sound simple, but it is a challenge to stay focussed on your key activities. I hope that you find these questions helpful. If you can answer them, you will be ready to launch your campaign.

One motivation for writing this book was observing over the last decade how these tools were useful to people across the world from democratic to more authoritarian contexts.

In South Africa, the 'but why?' technique helped NGOs to see that they did not have a full understanding of their issue, and that they needed to do some more research first. In Switzerland, work on the external environment showed campaigners that they did not all share the same understanding, and that they needed time to come to a common position. In Sudan the questions on research helped an NGO to see how they needed to develop their evidence base before they could begin to advocate for a change in government policy. In Senegal, the TEA test helped project staff see that they had in fact been campaigning for years - they just hadn't been calling it that! In Somaliland, the elevator test exercise was a revelation for local NGOs - they told me that they so often saw their target Minister in the market at the weekend, but were never quite sure what to say to him - this exercise ensured they were ready for the next opportunity!

In Ethiopia, the questions on risk were so important for NGO staff to help them to secure the support of their management. The influence tree has been an incredibly simple tool to help people think about whom they should seek to influence. In Haiti this tool led to a fascinating conversation about hidden power and the role of the Church, and that it is not always the government minister who has the power. And in the UK, the influence tree helped to show a group of lawyers that they did not actually know who had the power to make the change they wanted to see. Before using this tool, they would happily have launched a campaign with no focus on the real target!

In Peru, the opposition matrix enabled NGO staff from across Latin America to construct their campaign message firmly focussed on responding to the opposition arguments and made them change the framing of their messaging. In Germany, the theory of change tool enabled one international NGO to see that so much of their effort went into report writing and the subsequent press conference, and that they needed to invest more time into thinking about what happened next on their campaign. And in Bangladesh, the theory of change work helped an NGO to cope with setbacks on their campaign and to encourage them to think about different scenarios to seek to build influence.

Around the world, I have found a common problem that campaigners do not have a plan for success, and that they are always too busy to invest the time in reviewing their progress.

These simple and practical tools seem to have resonated around the world; and I hope, at least some of them, resonate with you.

But remember these questions are not a once in a lifetime exercise. Your answers should be reviewed on a regular basis. Your campaign will be engaging with human beings, with all of our varieties and eccentricities, and there will be many twists and turns.

For information on further reading and for the latest updates on my thinking and on current developments in campaigning do check out my website - http://jonathanelliscampaigns.com.

I have also developed on-line training courses to support this book on the Udemy training platform: https://www.udemy.com/user/jonathan-ellis-6/

So, maintain your focus, persistence, flexibility, and a burning desire to see change, remember why you are running your campaign, and don't lose sight of these questions and your answers, and look to build momentum on your issue . . . happy and successful campaigning!

Thanks for reading my book,

Jonathan

In summary

The key questions you need to answer before running an advocacy campaign

- What is campaigning and why is it important to you?
- What is your problem? But why is it a problem?
- Is there a common understanding of your external environment?
- What evidence have you got or do you need?
- Do you pass the TEA test?
- Can you do the elevator pitch?
- How credible are you and what are the risks?
- Do you know who your target is and how to reach them?
- How are you using opposition to help you?
- Have you got a theory of change?
- Have you got a plan for success?
- When are you next going to review progress?

Biography

Jonathan is an independent campaigner and teacher supporting charities and not-for-profits to campaign for change around the world – see http://jonathanelliscampaigns.com.

He also has developed online campaign training courses on the Udemy platform: https://www.udemy.com/user/jonathan-ellis-6

He has built a strong and successful track record of leading successful advocacy campaigns over the past 20 years. He led one of OXFAM GB's global campaigns, has led successful UK campaigns on refugee and housing issues, and until recently led policy, research and advocacy for the British Red Cross.

He has extensive experience supporting the development of advocacy campaigns across the world including: the Balkans, Bangladesh, Ethiopia, Haiti, Nigeria, Peru, Senegal, Somaliland, South Africa, Sudan, Tajikistan, Tanzania, Thailand and across Europe. He was also a visiting lecturer at City University in London on the MA in political communication from 2012-2015.

Among his voluntary roles, Jonathan is Chairman of the Bishop Simeon Trust (supporting orphans and vulnerable children in South Africa) and National Vice Chair of City of Sanctuary (helping to build a national movement in defence of asylum seekers and refugees).

Born in South Africa, he was educated at Durham (BA Hons History), Leicester (PGCE), Loughborough (MBA) and City (PG Certificate in Academic Practice) universities. He is a qualified teacher and a fellow of the Higher Education Academy.

Twitter: @JonathanMHEllis

27136457R00046

Printed in Great Britain
by Amazon